DITCH

THE UNCERTAINTY

Invest with Confidence in Emerging Markets: The Ultimate Guide to Business Risk Management and Investment Protection Treaties.

RUDSEL J. LUCAS

Name: Rudsel Julius Lucas

Title: Ditch the Uncertainty

Sub-title: An investor's guide to Investment Protection Treaties.

Description: The global investment landscape promises riches untold, but lurking beneath the surface are hidden dangers: political instability, murky regulations, and government actions that can vanish your capital faster than a magician's trick. But what if there was a hidden gem, a strategic location that unlocks a world of secure international investment opportunities? Ditch the uncertainty and unlock a world of secure investment opportunities. Make Curacao your secret weapon in the global investment arena.

We've poured our hearts into making this book a valuable resource for you. While the information is based on our research and experience, it's important to remember everyone's journey is unique.

This book is designed to spark ideas and offer different perspectives. We encourage you to adapt the methods presented to your own situation and consult with qualified professionals as needed.

First Edition 2024

Published by: Rudsel Julius Lucas (KDP Amazon)

A heartfelt salute to the dedicated professionals of Curaçao—past, present, and future. Your unwavering commitment and expertise have established Curaçao as a leading global hub for holding international investments.

CONTENTS

INTRODUCTION

Navigating the turbulent waters of emerging markets can often feel like a thrilling yet treacherous adventure. The lure of high returns is tempered by the risks associated with political instability, economic volatility, and regulatory unpredictability. How, then, can an investor safeguard their investments and still reap the potential rewards these markets offer? The answer lies in understanding and utilizing Investment Protection Treaties (IPTs).

The world of IPTs is complex, intricate, and often misunderstood. Yet, these treaties form a vital safety net, providing investors with legal protection against undue governmental interference, while also offering mechanisms for dispute resolution. They are a key tool in mitigating risk and providing the certainty needed to confidently invest in emerging markets.

"Ditch the Uncertainty" unravels the complexities of IPTs, offering a clear, concise, and comprehensive guide to these essential instruments. It provides the reader with a detailed understanding of the structure, function, and strategic use of

IPTs, and demystifies the legal jargon that often surrounds them.

Whether you are a seasoned investor seeking to broaden your investment horizons, or a novice venturing into emerging markets for the first time, this book serves as a crucial resource. It arms you with the knowledge and insights necessary to navigate the complexities of IPTs, enabling you to make informed decisions and protect your investments.

By shedding light on the role and significance of IPTs, this book encourages you to ditch the uncertainty that often accompanies investing in emerging markets. Instead, it empowers you to seize the opportunities these markets offer, backed by the security and confidence that comes with a thorough understanding of Investment Protection Treaties.

CHAPTER 1
NAVIGATING THE LABYRINTH:
INTRODUCTION TO IPTS

Mitigating Risk in Emerging Markets (Focus: Curaçao)

Investment Protection Treaties (IPTs) have emerged as crucial tools for mitigating risks and fostering investment in developing economies. These agreements establish a legal framework that protects foreign investors from arbitrary government actions, promotes fair and equitable treatment, and guarantees access to international arbitration in case of disputes.

Challenges and Opportunities in Emerging Markets

While emerging markets offer significant potential for investment returns, they also present unique challenges. Political instability, currency fluctuations, and weak legal systems can deter foreign investors. IPTs can help address these concerns by providing:

Stability and Predictability: IPTs establish clear rules and procedures for foreign investment, reducing uncertainty for investors.

Non-Discrimination: IPTs ensure that foreign investors are treated fairly and equally compared to domestic investors.

Dispute Settlement: IPTs provide a neutral forum for resolving investment disputes between foreign investors and host governments.

The Need for IPTs in Emerging Markets

The protection offered by IPTs can incentivize foreign investment, which is crucial for economic growth and development in emerging markets. By attracting foreign capital and expertise, emerging markets can create jobs, develop infrastructure, and improve technological advancements.

Curaçao's Advantage:

Curaçao's robust Bilateral Investment Treaty (BIT) network grants you:

- Stability: Peace of mind with a committed investment climate.

- Fair Play: Access to impartial international arbitration.

- Efficiency: Streamlined business setup and operation.

Leverage Curaçao's strategic location and strong IPT network to navigate emerging markets with confidence and unlock your international business potential.

Emerging Markets: Engines of Global Growth

The landscape of global economics is undergoing a dramatic transformation. As established powerhouses grapple with aging populations and slowing growth, a new breed of economic titans is rising on the horizon – emerging markets. These dynamic regions, once relegated to the fringes of the global financial map, are now blazing a path of rapid industrialization and exponential growth. They are the epicenters of economic metamorphosis, redefining the rules of global trade and investment, and shaping the future of business.

A Tapestry of Transformation

Emerging markets, often referred to as "developing economies" or "growth economies," encompass a diverse tapestry of nations at various stages of economic evolution. Powerhouses like India and China lead the pack, followed by countries like Brazil, Russia, South Africa, and the Southeast Asian tigers (Indonesia, Thailand, Vietnam). These regions are not merely experiencing a surge in economic output; they are undergoing a complete societal transformation. Infrastructure projects are booming, connecting remote villages to bustling metropolises. Educational institutions are churning out a skilled workforce hungry for opportunity. Socioeconomic fabrics are being rewoven, with burgeoning middle classes wielding newfound purchasing power.

A Goldmine of Opportunities

The significance of emerging markets lies in their sheer potential and the vast opportunities they present. Here are just a few of the compelling reasons why these regions are attracting global attention:

Untapped Consumer Base: Emerging markets boast a vast and largely untapped consumer base. With populations reaching into the billions and a burgeoning middle class experiencing a rise in disposable income, these regions present a goldmine for businesses and investors seeking new markets to penetrate and expand into. From consumer staples to cutting-edge technology, the demand for innovative products and services is immense.

Manufacturing Powerhouses: Competitive labor costs, coupled with rapidly improving infrastructure, are making emerging markets hubs for global manufacturing. This shift in the global supply chain presents a win-win situation. Businesses benefit from lower production costs, while emerging markets experience job creation and economic growth.

Resource Rich Havens: Emerging markets are often blessed with an abundance of natural resources, offering a wealth of opportunities for industries like energy, mining, and agriculture. From the vast oil reserves of Latin America to the fertile agricultural lands of sub-Saharan Africa, these regions hold the key to unlocking critical resources for the global economy.

Strategic Geographic Locations: Many emerging markets boast strategic geographic locations and diverse climates, making them attractive for various sectors like tourism, trade, and technology. From the bustling ports of Southeast Asia to the breathtaking landscapes of Africa, these regions offer unparalleled opportunities for businesses to expand their reach and tap into new markets.

The Engines of Future Growth

Perhaps the most crucial role of emerging markets lies in their potential to drive global economic growth. At a time when developed economies face headwinds like aging populations and sluggish growth, the dynamism and vitality of emerging markets are a welcome antidote. Their youthful demographics, high economic growth rates, and untapped potential position them as the engines of future global growth. As these economies mature and integrate further into the global economic system, they have the potential to lift millions out of poverty and create a more prosperous future for all.

Challenges and the Road Ahead

The path to prosperity for emerging markets is not without its challenges. Political instability, economic volatility, corruption, and inadequate infrastructure can stifle growth and deter investment. Regulatory frameworks and institutions are often evolving, posing risks and uncertainties for businesses and investors. However, these challenges are also opportunities in disguise. They demand innovative solutions, adaptable strategies, and a long-term vision. They necessitate a shift from purely profit-driven models towards sustainable and inclusive practices that benefit both businesses and local communities. Building strong partnerships, promoting responsible investment practices, and fostering good governance will be crucial in unlocking the full potential of these markets.

Embracing the Future

Emerging markets represent more than just lucrative investment destinations; they are the very crucible of change in the global economic landscape. Understanding their dynamics, harnessing their potential, and navigating the challenges they present will be crucial for navigating the future of global economics. By fostering collaboration, embracing innovation, and promoting sustainable practices, we can ensure that emerging markets truly become the engines of shared prosperity and a brighter economic future for all.

In today's world, uncertainty is unavoidable. It's a constant presence, weaving itself into every aspect of our lives, from personal decisions to global events. This complexity can feel overwhelming, a tangled web of unknowns that paralyzes us from taking action. But what if we reframed uncertainty, not as an enemy to be conquered, but as a challenge to be embraced?

A Tapestry of Influences

Uncertainty isn't a singular entity; it's a tapestry woven from multiple threads. Internal fears and doubts intertwine with external factors like societal shifts and technological advancements. This interplay creates a rich and dynamic picture, a constant dance between the familiar and the unknown.

Complexity as Opportunity

We often view complexity as negative, a hurdle to overcome. However, it can be a source of strength. Uncertainty fosters innovation, creativity, and the exploration of new possibilities. The key lies not in eliminating uncertainty, but in developing the skills to navigate its complexities.

Shifting Perspectives

Instead of fearing the labyrinth, we can learn to explore its many paths. Understanding complexity requires a shift in perspective. It's not about finding definitive answers, but about building awareness and developing a nuanced understanding.

A Holistic Approach

Uncertainty is interconnected. It's influenced by our internal world (perceptions, attitudes) and the external world (events, situations). Addressing it requires a holistic approach, acknowledging these interconnected elements.

A Dynamic Dance

The complexity of uncertainty isn't static; it's a dynamic dance subject to change. It evolves over time and varies across contexts. Understanding this dynamism allows us to be more adaptable and proactive in our approach.

Transforming Uncertainty

Grappling with complexity is a rewarding journey. By embracing the challenge of understanding uncertainty, we can transform it from a source of fear to a catalyst for growth and innovation. We can use it as a tool for personal and professional development.

Actionable Steps:

- While there's no one-size-fits-all solution, here are some practical steps to manage uncertainty:
- Identify Your Fears: Acknowledge your internal anxieties surrounding uncertainty.
- Gather Information: Research potential outcomes and gather as much information as possible.
- Develop Contingency Plans: Create flexible plans to address different scenarios.
- Focus on What You Can Control: Channel your energy into aspects you can influence.
- Embrace Openness: Be receptive to new information and adapt your approach as needed.

By understanding the complexity of uncertainty and taking these steps, we can not only survive but thrive in the face of the unknown. We can ditch the fear and embrace the empowering potential of uncertainty.

Why Investment Protection Treaties Matter

Investment Protection Treaties (IPTs) are often overlooked but play a crucial role in international trade and investment. These treaties establish a legal framework that safeguards foreign investors from unfair treatment by host governments. They provide stability, predictability, and a mechanism for resolving disputes, fostering a more attractive environment for foreign investment.

The Benefits of IPTs

Stability and Predictability: IPTs establish clear rules and procedures for foreign investment, reducing uncertainty for investors and encouraging long-term investment decisions.

Fair Treatment: IPTs ensure foreign businesses receive treatment equal to both domestic companies (National Treatment) and companies from any other country granted the most favorable terms (Most-Favored-Nation Treatment). This prevents discrimination and promotes a level playing field.

Dispute Settlement: IPTs provide a neutral forum for resolving investment disputes between foreign investors and host governments. This reduces the risk of lengthy and expensive litigation in local courts.

Protection from Expropriation: IPTs safeguard your investments from unfair seizure by the host government. Expropriation can only occur under exceptional circumstances with due process and fair compensation.

Guaranteed Repatriation: IPTs guarantee your ability to repatriate your investments and profits from the host country.

This ensures you can freely transfer your capital back home.

A Catalyst for Global Growth

By promoting stability, fair treatment, and dispute resolution mechanisms, IPTs act as a catalyst for global economic growth.

They encourage foreign investment, which can lead to:

- Job Creation: Increased foreign investment often translates to job creation in the host country.

- Economic Development: Foreign investment can spur economic growth by introducing new technologies, knowledge, and skills.

- Improved Infrastructure: Foreign investment can contribute to developing infrastructure projects, benefiting both businesses and local communities.

Beyond the Treaty

IPTs are just one piece of the puzzle for successful international investment. Careful due diligence, understanding the local market, and building strong relationships with local partners remain crucial for success.

Conclusion

In today's globalized world, Investment Protection Treaties play a vital role in promoting international trade and investment. By understanding the benefits and limitations of IPTs, investors can make informed decisions and navigate the complexities of the international market with greater confidence.

Secure Your Investments with IPTs

Considering an investment in an emerging market? Investment Protection Treaties (IPTs) offer vital safeguards for your business:

- Equal Treatment: Your company receives the same treatment as local businesses and those from other countries with favorable agreements.

- Seizure Protection: Your investment is protected from unfair government seizure.

- Profit Repatriation: You're guaranteed the ability to take your profits home.

- Efficient Fund Transfers: Moving funds across borders is streamlined.

Curacao as part of the The Kingdom of the Netherlands boasts a vast network of more than 100 BITs, significantly more than the US. This network extends to the Netherlands itself, as well as Aruba, Curaçao, and St. Maarten.

Protect your investments and unlock the full potential of emerging markets. Explore IPTs today!

CHAPTER 2
DEMYSTIFYING LAWS AND POLICIES

The Legal Landscape

The legal landscape can be a labyrinth, a complex web of laws and regulations that govern everything from our daily lives to international relations. Understanding this ever-changing system is crucial for making informed decisions and avoiding unnecessary risks.

A Dynamic System

Laws are not static pronouncements; they evolve with societal norms, technological advancements, and political shifts. Keeping up with these changes is a key challenge. New laws are enacted, existing ones are modified or repealed, and court decisions set new precedents. All this can significantly impact individuals, businesses, and society as a whole.

Vast and Complex

The legal landscape is vast and intricate, encompassing various fields with specialized knowledge. From criminal law and intellectual property to environmental regulations and corporate law, each area has its own unique set of rules and procedures.

Ambiguity and Opportunity

Laws can be open to interpretation, leading to uncertainty. However, this very ambiguity also presents opportunities. The legal framework provides a mechanism for resolving disputes, protecting rights, and promoting fairness. It allows businesses to operate with certainty and individuals to seek redress for wrongs.

Navigation Strategies

To navigate this complex system effectively, you don't need to be a legal scholar. Here are some tips:

- Identify Your Needs: Do you need basic legal information or assistance with a specific issue?

- Free Resources: Many government websites and legal aid organizations offer free legal information.

- Consult an Attorney: For complex issues, consider consulting a qualified lawyer specializing in your area of concern.

- Stay Informed: News outlets and legal blogs can help you stay abreast of legal developments.

The legal landscape, despite its complexities, is an essential part of a functioning society. By understanding its basic principles and employing these navigation strategies, you can make informed decisions, protect your rights, and take advantage of the opportunities the legal system offers. Remember, with knowledge and guidance, you can successfully navigate this ever-changing labyrinth.

Interpreting Policies

Demystifying Policy: A Guide to Interpretation

In the intricate world of policy, interpretation acts as a decoder ring, helping us understand the true meaning and implications of the rules that govern us. Policy interpretation is a crucial skill for navigating the complexities of decision-making and understanding the impact of different policy choices. This chapter delves into this vital skill, equipping you to navigate the complexities of policy interpretation.

Beyond the Words

Policy interpretation goes beyond simply understanding the literal meaning of a written document. It's about grasping the context, purpose, and potential impact of a policy. This requires a critical analysis of the wording, structure, and the underlying assumptions that shaped the policy. Think about who benefits, who might be disadvantaged, and how societal norms and economic realities influenced the policy's creation.

Adapting to Change

Policies are living documents, not static pronouncements. They evolve with changing times and circumstances. Effective interpretation requires flexibility and the ability to consider a policy's impact in the current context.

A Collaborative Effort

Policy interpretation isn't a solitary pursuit. It's a collaborative effort involving various stakeholders, including policymakers, businesses, citizen groups, and ordinary citizens. Each perspective enriches the interpretation process, leading to a more comprehensive understanding of the policy's implications.

Essential Tools

Several tools can aid in policy interpretation. The policy cycle model provides a framework for understanding the different stages of policy-making, from its creation to implementation. This model helps identify key players and factors influencing each stage.

Another valuable tool is the policy analysis matrix. This helps assess the potential costs and benefits of different policy options, highlighting potential winners and losers. By using this tool, policymakers can strive for more equitable and sustainable solutions.

A Moral Imperative

Policy interpretation is more than just an intellectual exercise; it's a moral and ethical responsibility. It involves evaluating the fairness, equity, and sustainability of a policy, particularly considering its impact on vulnerable populations. Effective interpretation requires a commitment to social justice, human rights, and environmental well-being.

Empowering Ourselves

In today's complex world, policy interpretation is an essential skill. By understanding how policies work, we can make informed decisions, challenge unjust policies, and advocate for change. It empowers us to shape a future that is fair, equitable, and sustainable. So, let's harness the power of policy interpretation and work together to create a better future for all.

Understanding the Fine Print

Demystifying the Fine Print: Your Key to Informed Decisions

Treasure maps may lead you to buried riches, but in the real world, valuable insights are often hidden within the cryptic language of the fine print. We've equipped you with tools to navigate uncertainty, but there's another layer to explore: the seemingly insignificant details that can trip you up if ignored. This section will guide you through understanding the fine print, those hidden clauses in contracts, agreements, and even online services that can transform a smooth journey into a frustrating maze.

Why the Fine Print Matters

The fine print isn't the enemy; it's an often overlooked instruction manual for navigating life's agreements. These details outline the terms and conditions, potential risks and benefits, and the responsibilities of all parties involved. Understanding them reduces uncertainty and empowers you to make informed decisions.

Consider a credit card agreement. The advertised interest rate might be attractive, but buried in the fine print could be hidden fees for exceeding your limit or late payments. This can turn a seemingly good deal into a financial burden.

Taking Control: A Four-Step Approach

Understanding the fine print isn't a one-time feat; it's an ongoing process. Here's a roadmap to navigate it effectively:

- Acknowledge Its Importance: Recognize that the fine print serves a purpose. It clarifies expectations and protects your interests.

- Embrace Patience: Don't skim through it. Take your time, research unfamiliar terms, and don't be afraid to ask questions.

- Seek Out Resources: The internet is your friend! Look up confusing terms, find explanations, or consult online resources.

- Consider seeking professional advice for complex situations.

- Put Knowledge into Action: Don't just understand the fine print, use that knowledge! Negotiate terms, clarify clauses, or even walk away from deals that don't align with your interests.

Understanding the fine print is an investment in your future. By equipping yourself with this knowledge, you can navigate life's uncertainties with greater confidence and make informed decisions that serve you well. So, the next time you encounter a lengthy document, don't shy away – decode the fine print and empower yourself!

Investment Protection Treaties Explained

Investment Protection Treaties (IPTs) act as a safety net for foreign investors, fostering a more secure environment for international investments. These legal agreements, established between nations, offer a range of protections, mitigating some of the inherent risks associated with investing abroad.

Key Features of IPTs

Protection from Expropriation: IPTs safeguard against government seizure of foreign-owned businesses or property without proper compensation.

Most-Favored-Nation Treatment (MFN): This clause ensures investors receive treatment equal to that of investors from any other country, promoting a level playing field.

Fair and Equitable Treatment (FET): This clause sets a standard of conduct for the host country, requiring fair treatment of foreign investors.

Dispute Resolution: IPTs often provide a mechanism for resolving investment disputes through international arbitration, offering a streamlined and impartial process.

Benefits and Limitations

While IPTs offer valuable protections, they are not a guarantee of success. Investors are still subject to host country laws and market fluctuations. Additionally, IPTs do not absolve investors of their social and environmental responsibilities.

Investment Protection Treaties play a vital role in the global investment landscape. They promote stability, fairness, and dispute resolution mechanisms, creating a more attractive environment for foreign investment. By understanding the features and limitations of IPTs, investors and policymakers can make informed decisions that contribute to a more prosperous global economy.

CHAPTER 3
A STEP–BY–STEP APPROACH

Getting Started

The opening chapter of "Ditch the Uncertainty" skillfully welcomes readers on a transformative journey of self-discovery. It acknowledges the inherent trepidation that often accompanies venturing into the unknown, particularly when it comes to confronting uncertainty. However, the chapter quickly assures readers that it serves as a guide, dispelling anxieties and equipping them with the tools to navigate this uncharted territory with greater confidence.

The chapter is portrayed as a rich resource, a treasure trove filled with valuable insights and practical exercises. These tools are designed to foster a deeper understanding of oneself and one's relationship with uncertainty. By peeling back the layers of ambiguity and fear, the chapter empowers readers to view uncertainty from a fresh perspective, recognizing it not as a roadblock, but as an opportunity for growth.

The core message is clear: the first step towards overcoming uncertainty lies in comprehension. The chapter delves into the nature of uncertainty, highlighting its influence on decisionmaking and risk-taking. Effectively framing uncertainty as a temporary state, rather than a permanent condition, fosters a sense of agency and control.

This shift in perspective is further emphasized by the use of a roadmap metaphor. The chapter is presented as a navigational tool, guiding readers through the labyrinth of uncertainty and emerging stronger, wiser, and more self-assured.

The focus on practical strategies is central to the chapter's appeal. It promises to equip readers with the tools to not only manage uncertainty but to transform it into a catalyst for positive change. The review concludes by reminding readers that significant journeys begin with a single step. This chapter serves as that initial step, urging readers to embrace the path towards a life free from doubt and brimming with confidence.

Risk Assessment

The second chapter of our transformative journey dives headfirst into the critical concept of Risk Assessment. This chapter sheds light on a process often relegated to the periphery, revealing its power to not only anticipate potential pitfalls but also to navigate life's uncertainties with greater confidence and control.

Risk Assessment transcends mere fortune-telling. It is a systematic approach, akin to a financial audit for your future endeavors. By systematically identifying potential risks, evaluating their impact, and formulating mitigation strategies, you gain a comprehensive understanding of the potential roadblocks that lie ahead. This knowledge empowers you to make informed decisions and chart a course that minimizes the impact of unforeseen circumstances.

The analogy of a road trip effectively underscores the practicality of Risk Assessment. Just as you wouldn't embark on a long journey without considering weather patterns and potential detours, a well-executed Risk Assessment equips you to anticipate life's storms and navigate through them more effectively. The focus here isn't on eliminating risks altogether, an unrealistic pursuit, but on understanding them, preparing for them, and minimizing their disruptive potential.

The chapter delves into the core steps of Risk Assessment. The first involves meticulous risk identification. This stage requires a comprehensive analysis of all potential threats, both readily apparent and those lurking beneath the surface. Financial considerations, health concerns, even relational hurdles and career uncertainties – all come under scrutiny. By taking a holistic approach, you gain a clear picture of the potential bumps along your path.

Following risk identification comes risk evaluation. Here, you analyze the potential impact of each identified threat. While some risks may cause minor inconveniences, others could significantly disrupt your plans. By meticulously evaluating each risk, you can prioritize your efforts, focusing on those with the greatest potential to derail your progress.

The final step culminates in risk management. This critical stage involves formulating strategies to address each identified threat. These strategies may involve implementing measures to reduce the likelihood of the risk occurring, or developing contingency plans to lessen its impact if it does materialize. This proactive approach transforms you from a passive observer to a capable navigator of life's uncertainties.

Risk Assessment isn't about succumbing to fear of the unknown. On the contrary, it empowers you with the knowledge and tools to navigate life's uncertainties with a newfound sense of agency. By understanding potential risks and developing mitigation strategies, you cultivate a sense of control and certainty in the face of the unknown.

Due Diligence

Venturing into the dynamic world of emerging markets can be exhilarating, promising high returns and exciting opportunities. However, this landscape also harbors hidden risks that can turn a promising investment sour. This is where due diligence, the cornerstone of informed investing, steps in.

The second chapter of our guide dives deep into the crucial practice of due diligence for emerging markets. It sheds light on a process that goes beyond mere financial analysis, revealing its power to illuminate potential pitfalls and empower investors to navigate these markets with greater confidence and control.

Due diligence transcends a simple check of the numbers. It's a systematic approach, akin to a comprehensive audit of a potential investment's future prospects. By meticulously identifying underlying risks, evaluating their potential impact, and formulating mitigation strategies, investors gain a holistic understanding of the potential challenges that lie ahead. This knowledge empowers them to make informed decisions and chart a course that minimizes the exposure to unforeseen circumstances.

Imagine entering a bustling marketplace in a new country. While the sights and sounds may be captivating, wouldn't you want to ensure the authenticity of the goods and the trustworthiness of the vendors before making a purchase? Due diligence serves a similar purpose. It equips investors to navigate the complexities of emerging markets and avoid hidden pitfalls.

The chapter delves into the core steps of effective due diligence. The first involves meticulous risk identification. This stage requires a comprehensive analysis of all potential threats, both readily apparent and those lurking beneath the surface. Political instability, currency fluctuations, legal ambiguities, and even social unrest – all come under scrutiny. By taking a holistic approach, investors gain a clear picture of the potential roadblocks that could derail their investment.

Following risk identification comes risk evaluation. Here, investors meticulously analyze the potential impact of each identified threat. While some risks may cause minor inconveniences, others could significantly disrupt the investment's profitability. By meticulously evaluating each risk, they can prioritize their concerns, focusing on those with the greatest potential to erode their returns.

The final step culminates in risk management. This critical stage involves formulating strategies to address each identified threat. These strategies may involve diversifying investments across different sectors, hedging against currency fluctuations, or establishing partnerships with local experts to navigate legal complexities. This proactive approach transforms investors from passive observers to capable navigators of emerging market uncertainties.

Due diligence isn't about succumbing to fear of the unknown. On the contrary, it empowers investors with the knowledge and tools to navigate emerging markets with a newfound sense of control. By understanding potential risks and developing mitigation strategies, they cultivate a sense of security and make informed decisions in the face of the unknown.

Investment Protection

As you delve into the dynamic world of emerging markets, an essential concept takes center stage: investment protection. It's not just about maximizing returns; it's about safeguarding your investments against potential risks and losses specific to these markets. This chapter equips you with a multi-layered approach, emphasizing not only robust investment protection strategies but also the critical role of legal structuring.

Imagine your investments venturing into uncharted territory, a land of exciting opportunities but also unforeseen challenges. Just as a seasoned explorer wouldn't embark on a journey without proper gear and knowledge, a savvy investor in emerging markets needs a comprehensive protection strategy. This chapter serves as your roadmap, guiding you through the essential tools and legal considerations to fortify your investments.

The first line of defense in your protection strategy should be diversification. Spreading your investments across a broad spectrum of asset classes, sectors, and geographical locations within the emerging market can mitigate the impact of unforeseen events. However, diversification alone may not be sufficient in emerging markets with unique legal and regulatory environments.

This is where legal structuring comes into play. Understanding and utilizing investment protection treaties (IPTs) becomes paramount. IPTs are international agreements between countries that establish a legal framework for foreign investments. By structuring your investments to qualify for protection under a relevant IPT, you gain access to international arbitration mechanisms in case of disputes with the host government. This empowers you to seek compensation for expropriation, unfair treatment, or breaches of investment guarantees.

The chapter will delve into the intricacies of identifying applicable IPTs, understanding their provisions, and structuring your investments to maximize their benefits. This knowledge empowers you to navigate complex legal landscapes and mitigate potential risks associated with government intervention.

Beyond legal structuring, the chapter explores other crucial investment protection strategies. Insurance products tailored to emerging market risks can provide a safety net. Stop-loss orders can help limit losses during market downturns, while asset allocation ensures your portfolio aligns with your risk tolerance and financial goals. Regular portfolio reviews and rebalancing are essential for maintaining your desired level of protection and maximizing growth potential.

Remember, investment protection isn't about eliminating risk entirely. It's about managing it effectively. By combining a well-diversified investment strategy with a legally sound structure, you build a robust defense for your investments in emerging markets. This chapter equips you with the knowledge and tools to navigate this exciting yet complex landscape, empowering you to move closer to your financial goals with greater confidence and control.

CHAPTER 4
PRACTICAL ADVICE FOR RISK MANAGEMENT

Identifying Risks

The first step in eliminating uncertainty is to pinpoint the potential hazards that may lurk in the shadows of your path. This process, known as risk identification, is crucial in any endeavour, be it business, personal, or otherwise. The ability to foresee potential pitfalls allows you to plan and prepare adequately, thereby reducing the element of uncertainty.

Risk identification is not a process that should be rushed. It is a meticulous exercise that requires an in-depth understanding of your environment, your capabilities, and your limitations. To identify risks, you must first assess the landscape in which you operate. This includes understanding the external factors that may influence your operations such as economic conditions, legal regulations, technological advancements, and market trends. These factors may present risks in the form of regulatory changes, economic downturns, or disruptive technologies.

In addition to external factors, internal risks must also be considered. These may include operational risks such as system failures, human errors, or a lack of skilled personnel. Strategic risks such as a poor business strategy or a lack of competitive advantage may also be present. Financial risks such as inadequate funding or poor financial management can also pose significant threats.

Identifying risks requires a thorough examination of all aspects of your operations. It requires you to question every assumption, challenge every norm, and scrutinize every decision. It is a process that demands critical thinking and a willingness to confront uncomfortable truths.

Once risks have been identified, they must be documented. This documentation should include a detailed description of the risk, the potential impact it may have, and any mitigating factors that may reduce its likelihood or impact. This will serve as a valuable reference tool for future risk management activities.

It is also important to remember that risk identification is not a one-time activity. As your environment changes, new risks may emerge while others may become obsolete. Therefore, risk identification should be an ongoing process, with regular reviews and updates to ensure that your risk profile remains accurate and up-to-date.

Risk identification may seem like a daunting task. It may seem easier to ignore potential risks and hope for the best. However, by doing so, you are merely trading short-term comfort for long-term uncertainty. By identifying risks, you are taking the first step towards reducing uncertainty and gaining control over your future.

In the end, the process of identifying risks is not about predicting every possible obstacle or setback. Instead, it is about developing a deep understanding of your environment and your operations. It is about recognizing the potential pitfalls that may lie ahead and preparing for them. By doing so, you can navigate your path with greater confidence, knowing that you are ready to face whatever challenges may come your way.

Remember, uncertainty is not a sign of weakness or a lack of planning. It is a natural part of life and business. However, by identifying risks, you can transform uncertainty from a source of fear into a source of strength. You can turn it from a stumbling block into a stepping stone, from a threat into an opportunity. And in doing so, you can ditch the uncertainty and embrace the possibilities that lie ahead.

Mitigating Risks

In the realm of uncertainty, the ability to curb potential threats and reduce risks is a crucial skill. It is about taking a proactive approach rather than being reactive. The process often involves identifying potential risks, analyzing them, and then taking the necessary steps to reduce or eliminate them.

To initiate this process, the first step is to recognize the risks. This might sound straightforward, but it's often the most overlooked step. You can't mitigate risks if you can't identify them. To do this, one must have a deep understanding of their business, market, and environment. This includes a clear understanding of your business model, your market position, your competition, and the overall industry trends.

Once you have identified the risks, the next step is to evaluate them. This involves assessing the likelihood of each risk eventuating, and the potential impact it could have on your business. The purpose of this step is to prioritize the risks based on their severity. Not all risks are created equal, and you need to focus your efforts on the ones that could cause the most damage.

Having identified and evaluated the risks, the next course of action is to develop strategies to mitigate them. There are several methods you can employ. One common approach is to avoid the risk. This could involve changing your business strategy or process to ensure the risk does not eventuate. Another approach is to reduce the risk. This could involve implementing new procedures or controls to diminish the likelihood or impact of the risk.

A third approach is to share the risk. This could involve entering into partnerships or contracts that share the risk with other parties. Lastly, you could choose to accept the risk. This is typically done when the cost of mitigating the risk outweighs the potential benefit. In such cases, it's important to have a contingency plan in place should the risk eventuate.

While the steps above provide a framework for mitigating risks, it's important to note that risk management is not a one-time event. It's an ongoing process that needs to be integrated into your business strategy and operations. It's about creating a culture of risk awareness and management within your organization. This involves training your staff to identify and respond to risks, and creating open channels of communication where risks can be reported and discussed.

It's also important to regularly review and update your risk management strategies. Risks can change over time, and your strategies need to evolve to stay effective. This might involve updating your risk identification and evaluation processes, or adjusting your mitigation strategies based on new information or changes in your business environment.

In the face of uncertainty, risk mitigation is your best defense. It's about taking control of the situation, and turning uncertainty into certainty. It's about making informed decisions, rather than leaving things to chance. By adopting a proactive approach to risk management, you can not only safeguard your business but also seize new opportunities that come your way.

Risk Management Strategies

Navigating through the turbulent waters of uncertainty, one must be equipped with the right set of tools to mitigate the potential risks. The art of managing risks is not a mere act, but a strategy that requires careful planning, execution, and monitoring. This section will delve into the various strategies that can be employed to effectively manage risks and reduce the impact of uncertainty.

Risk management strategies are essentially a series of steps that are taken to identify, assess, and prioritize risks followed by the application of resources to minimize, monitor, and control the probability or impact of unfortunate events. The strategies can be broadly categorized into four types: avoidance, reduction, sharing, and retention.

Avoidance strategy, as the name suggests, involves steering clear of the risky activity. If the potential loss from the risk outweighs the anticipated benefits, it may be wiser to avoid the risk. This could mean not investing in a particular market, not launching a new product, or even not undertaking a potentially harmful project.

Reduction strategy is about minimizing the impact of risk. This can be achieved by implementing robust systems and processes, investing in research and development, or maintaining stringent quality controls. For instance, a company could reduce the risk of product failure by investing in extensive product testing and quality assurance.

Sharing the risk is another strategy often used, especially when the potential loss is too significant for one entity to bear. This could involve sharing the risk with other businesses, or transferring the risk to an insurance company. For example, a company may choose to insure its assets to mitigate the risk of loss due to theft or damage.

Retention is the strategy used when the cost of managing the risk is more than the cost of the risk itself. This means accepting the risk and establishing a contingency plan to deal with it if it occurs. For instance, a business may decide to retain the risk of a new product launch, accepting that there may be initial losses.

These strategies are not mutually exclusive and can be used in combination for effective risk management. For instance, a company may choose to avoid some risks, reduce others, share some, and retain a few. The choice of strategy would depend on the nature of the risk, the potential impact, and the cost of managing the risk.

It is important to note that risk management is not a one-time activity, but a continuous process. It involves regular monitoring and review of the risks and the effectiveness of the strategies used to manage them. This would involve regular risk assessments, audits, and reviews.

Monitoring and managing risks is a proactive approach to dealing with uncertainty. It enables businesses to anticipate potential risks and take appropriate action to mitigate them.

This not only reduces the impact of the risks but also provides the business with a competitive advantage.

While it is not possible to eliminate all risks, effective risk management strategies can help in significantly reducing the uncertainty and the potential damage it can cause. By identifying, assessing, and managing risks, businesses can not only survive but thrive in the uncertain world of business.

Risk management strategies are not just about dealing with potential threats, but also about identifying and exploiting opportunities. It is about making informed decisions, taking calculated risks, and ensuring the sustainability and success of the business. So, ditch the uncertainty, embrace the strategies, and sail through the turbulent waters of business with confidence and control.

Staying Ahead of the Game

A swift, relentless current of change defines the modern world. The pace is unyielding, demanding agility and adaptability from those who wish to succeed. To thrive in such an environment, one must not only keep up but stay ahead. The rules of the game are perpetually in flux, and falling behind can mean being swept away. Therefore, it is crucial to maintain a proactive stance, to anticipate shifts before they occur, and to adjust one's strategy accordingly. This is the essence of staying ahead of the game.

Consider the world of business, a sphere where change is not just constant but rapid and often transformative. New technologies, evolving market dynamics, changing consumer preferences, and regulatory shifts are just a few of the factors that can upturn established norms and paradigms overnight. In such a landscape, businesses that cling to outdated practices or fail to anticipate these shifts often find themselves struggling to catch up, while those that are agile and forward-looking thrive.

To stay ahead of the game, one must nurture an environment of continuous learning and improvement. This entails staying abreast of new developments in one's field, actively seeking out opportunities for growth, and cultivating a mindset that views change not as a threat but an opportunity. It also means being willing to take calculated risks, to venture into uncharted territory when the potential rewards justify it.

Staying ahead of the game also requires a keen understanding of one's environment. This involves closely monitoring the competitive landscape, identifying emerging trends, and understanding the implications of broader societal and economic shifts. It means being attuned to subtle shifts in the wind, and being ready to adjust one's sails accordingly. This level of strategic awareness is not easy to cultivate, but it is invaluable in navigating an ever-changing landscape.

One of the key elements in staying ahead of the game is innovation. Those who innovate create their own path, setting the pace rather than following it. They are the game changers, the ones who redefine the rules and shape the future. Innovation, however, is not just about coming up with new ideas or products. It's also about finding new ways to do things, new ways to solve problems, new ways to deliver value. It's about thinking differently, challenging the status quo, and daring to do things differently.

Resilience, too, is a crucial ingredient in staying ahead of the game. The path forward is rarely smooth or straight, and setbacks are inevitable. Those who stay ahead are those who can weather these storms, who can pick themselves up after a fall and keep moving forward. They are persistent and tenacious, undeterred by obstacles and undaunted by challenges.

In the final analysis, staying ahead of the game is about being proactive rather than reactive, about leading rather than following. It's about understanding that change is not something to be feared but embraced, not something to be resisted but harnessed. It's about being prepared, being adaptable, being resilient, and above all, being ready to seize the opportunities that change brings. This is the path to not just surviving, but thriving in a world of uncertainty.

CHAPTER 5
DUE DILIGENCE: A DEEP DIVE

The Importance of Due Diligence

There is a certain level of uncertainty that accompanies any endeavor, especially in the world of business. This uncertainty can stem from a variety of sources, be it the volatility of the market, the unpredictability of consumer behavior, or the everpresent threat of competition. However, one area where uncertainty should never be allowed is in the process of decision-making. This is where the concept of due diligence comes into play.

Due diligence, in its essence, is the process of thoroughly researching and understanding all aspects of a decision before it is made. It is the act of gathering all relevant information and analyzing it to make the most informed decision possible. It is the difference between diving headfirst into unknown waters and carefully testing the depth and temperature before taking the plunge.

In the world of business, due diligence is not just a good practice, it is a necessity. It is the shield that protects businesses from making poorly informed decisions that could lead to financial loss, legal issues, and reputational damage. It is the compass that guides businesses through the complex maze of decision-making, helping them avoid potential pitfalls and reach their desired destination.

The importance of due diligence can be seen in various aspects of business. For instance, when considering an investment, due diligence involves scrutinizing the financial health of the company, understanding its business model, assessing the competence of its management team, and evaluating its market position and growth potential. It is a rigorous process that requires time, effort, and expertise, but it is absolutely crucial in mitigating investment risk.

Similarly, in the realm of mergers and acquisitions, due diligence is the backbone of the process. It involves examining every facet of the target company, from its financial statements and assets to its legal obligations and potential liabilities. It is a thorough investigation that aims to uncover any hidden issues or risks that could affect the value of the deal.

In the context of hiring, due diligence involves conducting background checks, verifying qualifications, and assessing the potential fit of the candidate with the company culture. It is a crucial step in ensuring that the right people are brought onboard, people who can contribute positively to the company's growth and success.

The process of due diligence, while time-consuming and sometimes tedious, is a critical step in mitigating uncertainty. It provides a solid foundation upon which decisions can be made with confidence. It allows businesses to move forward, not with blind faith, but with a clear vision of the potential risks and rewards that lie ahead.

In essence, due diligence is the antidote to uncertainty. It is the tool that allows businesses to navigate the unpredictable waters of the business world with confidence and precision. It is the process that empowers businesses to ditch the uncertainty, to make informed decisions, and to ultimately achieve success.

Therefore, the importance of due diligence cannot be overstated. It is not an optional extra, but rather an essential part of any successful business strategy. It is the key to turning uncertainty into certainty, risk into reward, and potential pitfalls into opportunities for growth and success.

Conducting Due Diligence

In the realm of business, the phrase 'due diligence' often echoes in the corridors of decision-making. An essential process, it is a rigorous investigation into a potential investment or product to validate all facts. It includes reviewing all financial records, plus anything else deemed material. It is the safety net that saves businesses from making misguided decisions, ensuring that all stones are turned and every potential pitfall or opportunity is brought to light.

This process of conducting due diligence is as critical as the decision to invest itself. It is the path that leads to a wellinformed and rational decision. It can be seen as the bridge between uncertainty and certainty, offering a clear, detailed appraisal of the potential investment or product.

The first step in this process is to understand what due diligence is. It is not about just ticking off boxes or going through the motions. Instead, it is about plumbing the depths of the proposed investment, understanding its structure, operations, financial health, market position, and potential risks and returns. The aim is to gather as much information as possible to make an informed decision.

The scope of due diligence is vast. It covers every aspect of the business. Financial due diligence looks at the financial health of the business. It involves a thorough review of financial statements, projections, capital structure, revenue streams, and cost structures. It also looks at financial compliance, tax liabilities, and any potential financial risks.

Operational due diligence, on the other hand, looks at the operations of the business. It involves reviewing operational processes, supply chains, technology, human resources, and infrastructure. It seeks to understand the efficiency and effectiveness of the operations and identify any potential operational risks or opportunities.

Legal due diligence is another critical aspect. It involves reviewing all legal aspects of the business, including contracts, leases, licenses, intellectual property, litigation, and legal compliance. It aims to identify any potential legal risks or liabilities.

Market due diligence involves a comprehensive analysis of the market in which the business operates. It looks at market size, trends, competition, customer behavior, and regulatory environment. It seeks to understand the business's market position and potential for growth.

The process of conducting due diligence is systematic and structured. It starts with a due diligence checklist, which outlines all the information needed. The information is then gathered through various means, including document reviews, interviews, site visits, and third-party investigations. The information is then analyzed, and a due diligence report is prepared, providing a detailed appraisal of the potential investment or product.

The value of conducting due diligence cannot be overstated. It is the process that uncovers the hidden aspects of the business, providing a clear picture of what lies beneath the surface. It is the process that helps businesses to ditch the uncertainty and make well-informed decisions.

However, conducting due diligence is not without challenges. It requires time, resources, and expertise. It also requires a willingness to dig deep and question everything. But despite these challenges, it is a necessary process, one that can save businesses from costly mistakes and help them seize valuable opportunities.

In the world of business, where uncertainty is a constant companion, conducting due diligence is the beacon of light that guides the way. It is the process that helps businesses navigate the murky waters of decision-making, leading them to the shores of certainty.

Key Areas to Investigate

In the realm of uncertainty, there are certain domains that must be thoroughly explored to gain a comprehensive understanding of the subject matter. These key areas of investigation not only provide a more in-depth insight into the nature of uncertainty, but they also offer a roadmap to navigate through the foggy landscape of unpredictability.

The first area of investigation involves understanding the origin of uncertainty. Uncertainty is like a seed that sprouts from various sources. It can be born out of lack of knowledge, ambiguity in communication, or unpredictability of future events. Grasping the roots of uncertainty helps in devising effective strategies to manage it. A deep dive into its source can reveal if it's an inherent part of the situation or a product of our own thought processes. This understanding can empower us to either confront the situation more effectively or change our perspective towards it.

The second area of focus should be the impact of uncertainty. Uncertainty, in its many forms, can have a profound effect on our emotional, cognitive, and behavioral responses. It can induce stress, anxiety, and fear, impair decision-making abilities, and even lead to paralysis by analysis. Investigating the impact of uncertainty helps in recognizing its symptoms and understanding the toll it takes on our mental health. This awareness can prompt us to seek help when needed and take proactive steps to mitigate the adverse effects of uncertainty.

The third area to explore is our individual response to uncertainty. Each one of us has a unique way of dealing with uncertainty, shaped by our experiences, beliefs, and personality traits. Some might react with panic and fear, while others might see it as an opportunity for growth and learning. Delving into our personal response patterns enables us to identify the strengths and weaknesses of our coping mechanisms. This selfawareness can lead to self-improvement, as we learn to cultivate resilience, adaptability, and flexibility in the face of uncertainty.

The fourth area involves examining the strategies to manage uncertainty. There are numerous tools and techniques, ranging from mindfulness and cognitive restructuring to scenario planning and risk management, which can help in dealing with uncertainty. Investigating these strategies provides us with a toolkit to handle the unpredictable twists and turns of life. The more strategies we have at our disposal, the better equipped we are to confront uncertainty.

The fifth and final area of investigation pertains to the potential benefits of uncertainty. Yes, you read it right. Uncertainty, despite its reputation, is not entirely detrimental. It can spur creativity, foster learning, and promote personal growth. It makes us question our assumptions, pushes us out of our comfort zones, and forces us to adapt and evolve. Exploring this aspect of uncertainty can help us appreciate its value and see it in a new light.

In the quest to ditch uncertainty, these key areas of investigation act as guiding stars. They illuminate the path, provide valuable insights, and equip us with the necessary tools to navigate the murky waters of uncertainty. By delving deep into these areas, we can transform uncertainty from a daunting challenge into an opportunity for growth and learning.

Overcoming Due Diligence Challenges

As we navigate the complex world of due diligence, we encounter numerous challenges that can often seem insurmountable. However, it is essential to remember that these obstacles are not roadblocks but rather stepping stones on the path to achieving successful due diligence. Overcoming these challenges requires a robust strategy, a clear understanding of the process, and a willingness to adapt and evolve.

Firstly, let's consider the issue of information overload. In the era of digital technology, we are inundated with data. While this wealth of information can be beneficial, it can also be overwhelming and lead to confusion and indecision. The solution lies in having a structured approach to data management. Using advanced analytical tools and techniques can help sift through the noise and identify the information that is truly relevant and valuable. It is also crucial to continuously update and refine our data management strategies to keep pace with evolving technologies and trends.

Secondly, there is the issue of time constraints. Due diligence is a time-consuming process, and time is often a scarce resource in business. The key to overcoming this challenge is efficient project management. Developing a detailed project plan, setting realistic timelines, and allocating resources effectively can significantly reduce the time required for due diligence. Moreover, integrating technology into the process can automate repetitive tasks and free up time for more critical aspects of due diligence.

Thirdly, we have the challenge of dealing with uncertainty. The future is unpredictable, and even the most thorough due diligence cannot eliminate all risks. However, this does not mean that we should shy away from uncertainty. Instead, we should learn to manage it. This involves recognizing, acknowledging, and understanding the risks involved and developing strategies to mitigate them. It also involves being prepared for different scenarios and having contingency plans in place.

Fourthly, there is the challenge of cultural differences. In an increasingly globalized world, due diligence often involves dealing with businesses from different cultures. This can lead to misunderstandings and conflicts, which can derail the due diligence process. Overcoming this challenge requires cultural sensitivity and understanding. It involves learning about different cultures, understanding their business practices and norms, and adapting our communication and negotiation strategies accordingly.

Lastly, there is the challenge of regulatory compliance. Laws and regulations vary across different jurisdictions, and noncompliance can lead to severe penalties. Overcoming this challenge requires a thorough understanding of the relevant laws and regulations. It also requires regular monitoring and updating of our compliance strategies to ensure they remain relevant and effective.

Overcoming these due diligence challenges is not an easy task. It requires patience, perseverance, and a lot of hard work. But with the right strategies and tools, it is achievable. And the rewards – a successful due diligence process, a sound investment decision, and ultimately, business success – are well worth the effort. Remember, the road to success is always under construction. So, let's roll up our sleeves and get to work!

CHAPTER 6
DISPUTE RESOLUTION: STRATEGIES AND SOLUTIONS

Understanding Disputes

Disputes, in their myriad forms, are an inevitable part of life. They can occur in various contexts and scales, ranging from minor squabbles between friends to major conflicts between nations. The fundamental essence of a dispute lies in a disagreement or difference of opinion. However, it is imperative to understand that disputes are not merely about opposing views, but involve a complex interplay of emotions, perceptions, and interests.

Disputes can be seen as the manifestation of underlying uncertainties. These uncertainties could revolve around unmet needs, unrealized expectations, or unfulfilled promises. They could be about the interpretation of facts, the application of rules, or the assessment of behavior. They could stem from the fear of loss, the desire for gain, or the quest for justice. Whatever the source, uncertainties fuel disputes by creating ambiguity and tension, and by challenging the status quo.

At their core, disputes are about communication, or more specifically, the lack thereof. They arise when parties fail to effectively convey their thoughts, feelings, and intentions to one another. They persist when parties refuse to listen to each other, or when they misinterpret or distort what is being said. They escalate when parties resort to aggressive tactics, such as blaming, threatening, or manipulating, instead of engaging in constructive dialogue.

To understand disputes, it is also crucial to recognize their dynamic nature. They do not occur in a vacuum, but are influenced by a range of external factors. These may include cultural norms, social pressures, economic conditions, and political dynamics. Furthermore, disputes evolve over time, as parties adjust their positions, strategies, and goals based on their experiences and perceptions. This dynamism adds another layer of complexity to disputes, making them challenging to manage and resolve.

Disputes are not inherently negative. They can serve as a catalyst for change, prompting parties to re-examine their beliefs, values, and behaviors. They can stimulate creativity and innovation, as parties seek novel solutions to their problems. They can foster personal growth and transformation, as parties learn to deal with adversity, develop empathy, and build resilience.

However, disputes can also have negative consequences. They can cause stress, anxiety, and depression, damage relationships, and disrupt social harmony. They can lead to violence, destruction, and loss, and can even trigger wars and revolutions. Hence, it is critical to manage and resolve disputes effectively, to minimize their negative impacts and maximize their positive potential.

Understanding disputes is the first step towards managing and resolving them. This requires a holistic approach, which considers not only the overt issues, but also the underlying uncertainties, the communication dynamics, and the external influences. It also requires a reflective approach, which encourages parties to introspect on their own roles, biases, and assumptions in the dispute.

In essence, disputes are complex, dynamic, and multifaceted phenomena. They are a reflection of the uncertainties inherent in human interactions. To navigate through them, one must ditch the fear of the unknown, embrace the diversity of perspectives, and embark on a journey of understanding, empathy, and collaboration.

Preventing Disputes

Striving for harmony and understanding in relationships, whether personal or professional, is a universal aim. However, the path to achieving this is often littered with disputes of varying severity. The key to minimizing these disagreements lies not in the resolution, but in prevention. This subchapter will guide you through the art of preventing disputes, thereby eliminating the uncertainty that often accompanies conflict resolution.

The first step to dispute prevention is fostering open communication. This entails not only speaking clearly and honestly but also actively listening to what others have to say. By creating an environment where everyone feels heard and understood, the likelihood of misunderstandings leading to disputes is significantly reduced.

Additionally, setting clear expectations is crucial. When everyone involved knows what is expected of them, there is less room for misinterpretation, which is a common cause of disputes. This could be as simple as laying out the details of a project at work, or as complex as discussing the parameters of a personal relationship.

Further, it is imperative to respect differences. Disputes often arise from a lack of understanding or acceptance of others' perspectives. Recognize that each person brings a unique viewpoint to the table, and these differences are not a hindrance but a strength. By acknowledging and appreciating these differences, you pave the way for mutual respect and hence, fewer disputes.

It is also essential to develop emotional intelligence, which is the ability to understand and manage your emotions and those of others.

This skill can help you to perceive when a dispute might be brewing and allow you to address the issue before it escalates.

Another effective strategy for preventing disputes is to engage in regular feedback sessions. These provide an opportunity for all parties to express concerns or grievances before they turn into significant disputes. These sessions should be conducted in a non-confrontational manner, focusing on problem-solving rather than blame.

Moreover, the practice of empathy cannot be overstated. Putting yourself in the shoes of another person allows you to understand their perspective better, minimizing the chances of a dispute. This does not mean you have to agree with their viewpoint, but understanding it can help prevent disagreements from escalating.

Proactive conflict prevention also involves creating and maintaining a positive environment. This can be achieved by encouraging teamwork, promoting equality, and discouraging gossip or other negative behaviors. A positive environment can prevent minor disagreements from escalating into major disputes.

Finally, it is important to remember that preventing disputes does not mean avoiding conflict altogether. Conflict, when managed effectively, can lead to growth and innovation. The goal of dispute prevention is not to create a conflict-free zone, but to cultivate a space where conflicts can be dealt with constructively and without escalating into damaging disputes.

In the quest to ditch uncertainty, the focus should not just be on solving disputes, but also on preventing them from arising in the first place. This requires a proactive approach and the adoption of strategies aimed at fostering open communication, setting clear expectations, respecting differences, developing emotional intelligence, providing regular feedback, practicing empathy, and maintaining a positive environment. By doing so, you can create a space where disputes are few and far between, and uncertainty becomes a thing of the past.

Resolving Disputes

When disagreements arise, as they inevitably will, the path to resolution can often seem shrouded in fog. It is the human condition to have differing perspectives, opinions, and interpretations. However, it is through the resolution of these disputes that we gain clarity, understanding, and ultimately, progress.

The dispute resolution process is a dance, a delicate interplay of communication, negotiation, and mutual respect. It is not a battle to be won, but a conversation to be navigated. It begins with understanding, both of the dispute at hand and of the individuals involved.

Understanding the dispute requires a deep dive into the subject matter, the context, and the implications. It requires an objective analysis of the facts, a critical evaluation of the evidence, and a comprehensive understanding of the potential outcomes. This understanding forms the foundation upon which the resolution process is built.

Understanding the individuals involved in the dispute is just as important. Each person brings their own perspectives, experiences, and biases to the table. Recognizing these factors and accounting for them in the resolution process is crucial. It involves active listening, empathy, and patience. This understanding helps to build trust, foster communication, and facilitate negotiation.

Negotiation is the heart of the dispute resolution process. It is where the parties come together to find a solution that is acceptable to all. It is a delicate balancing act of give and take, compromise and concession. It requires flexibility, creativity, and a willingness to see beyond one's own position. It requires the ability to identify common ground, to build on it, and to use it as a platform for resolution.

Communication is the lifeblood of negotiation. It is through communication that understanding is built, that perspectives are shared, that solutions are proposed. Effective communication involves not only speaking clearly and persuasively, but also listening attentively and respectfully. It involves not only expressing one's own position, but also understanding and acknowledging the other's. It involves not only advocating for one's own interests, but also finding ways to accommodate the other's.

Respect is the glue that binds the dispute resolution process together. It is the recognition of the other's worth and dignity, the acknowledgment of their right to have differing opinions, the affirmation of their role in the resolution process. Respect fosters trust, encourages communication, and facilitates negotiation. It diffuses tension, reduces animosity, and promotes cooperation.

The path to dispute resolution may not be easy, but it is always possible. It requires effort, patience, and a commitment to understanding, negotiation, communication, and respect. It requires the willingness to set aside preconceptions, to see beyond differences, to find common ground. It is a journey of discovery, of learning, of growth.

Dispute resolution is not about winning or losing. It is about finding a solution that respects all parties involved, that addresses the issue at hand, and that paves the way for future cooperation and understanding. It is about ditching the uncertainty, embracing the possibilities, and moving forward together. It is about transforming disputes into opportunities for growth, understanding, and progress.

Learning from Past Disputes

Within the realm of human interactions, conflicts and disputes are an inevitable reality. Our past is riddled with disagreements, both minor and major, personal and professional. These past disputes, however, are not mere memories to be forgotten, but rather, valuable lessons to be learned from. The purpose of this chapter is to shed light on the importance of learning from past disputes and how such learning can help us ditch the uncertainty.

Firstly, past disputes are rich mines of lessons about human behavior and communication. They offer insights into what triggers conflict, how people react under stress, and how different strategies can either escalate or diffuse tension. By analyzing past disputes, we can understand the patterns and predict future behavior, thereby reducing the uncertainty in our interactions. We can anticipate potential triggers and avoid them, understand the other person's perspective better, and choose the right communication strategies to prevent misunderstandings.

Moreover, past disputes also help us understand ourselves better. They make us aware of our own triggers, our reactions under stress, our communication style, and our conflict resolution skills. This self-awareness is crucial in managing future conflicts.

We can work on our weaknesses, improve our communication and negotiation skills, and become more effective in dealing with disagreements. This not only reduces uncertainty but also boosts our confidence and self-esteem.

Learning from past disputes is not just about understanding human behavior and improving skills. It is also about healing and moving on. Sometimes, disputes leave deep scars, affecting our relationships and mental health. By revisiting these incidents and learning from them, we can find closure and let go of the past. We can forgive ourselves and others, rebuild damaged relationships, and move forward with a positive mindset. This process of healing is essential in ditching the uncertainty and embracing a future free from the shadows of past conflicts.

However, learning from past disputes is not always easy. It requires courage to face our mistakes and weaknesses, humility to accept our faults, and wisdom to see the bigger picture. It requires the willingness to change, to improve, and to let go. But the rewards of this process are immense. It not only empowers us to handle future conflicts more effectively but also enriches our relationships and personal growth.

In the context of professional disputes, learning from the past is equally important. It helps organizations develop effective conflict management strategies, build a positive work culture, and improve team dynamics. It enables leaders to manage their teams more effectively, foster open communication, and promote mutual respect and understanding. By learning from past disputes, organizations can ditch the uncertainty and create a productive and harmonious work environment.

To sum up, past disputes are not just unpleasant memories to be buried, but valuable lessons to be learned from. They are opportunities for personal and professional growth, for improving relationships, and for building a future free from uncertainty. So let's not shy away from our past disputes. Instead, let's analyze them, learn from them, and use them as stepping stones to a future of certainty and confidence. Remember, it's not the disputes that define us, but how we learn from them and move forward.

CHAPTER 7
POWER OF REAL—WORLD CASE STUDIES

Case Study Analysis

The essence of uncertainty is deeply ingrained in our everyday life, leading us down paths of indecision and hesitation. While it is inherently human to experience such feelings, the information shared in this book "Ditch the Uncertainty" encourages its readers to break free from this cycle, offering practical strategies to conquer this often debilitating state of mind. By closely examining real-life case studies, the book provides an insightful analysis of how individuals have successfully managed to navigate through the murky waters of uncertainty.

One compelling case study revolves around Sarah, a mid-level manager in a multinational corporation. She was constantly plagued by uncertainty, doubting her decisions and secondguessing her actions. The resultant stress and anxiety started taking a toll on her professional and personal life. The book explores how Sarah managed to overcome these challenges by implementing the strategies suggested within its pages.

The book delves into Sarah's transformation and use it as guidance to, provide a detailed account of her journey. Initially, she was skeptical about the effectiveness of the proposed strategies. However, as she started implementing them, she began to notice a marked difference in her thought process. She started questioning her insecurities instead of her decisions, which was a significant shift in her mindset. This shift was the first step towards overcoming uncertainty.

The book also explores the case study of Mark, a small business owner who was always uncertain about his business decisions. He was constantly worried about the future of his business, which affected his risk-taking ability. The book describes how Mark managed to ditch the uncertainty by adopting a more positive and confident approach towards his business decisions.

By using Mark's journey as guidance, the book highlights the importance of confidence in decision-making. It shows how Mark, who was once afraid of taking risks, started making confident decisions that ultimately led to the growth of his business. This transformation was possible because Mark decided to trust his instincts and capabilities, thereby ditching the uncertainty.

The book uses these case studies to highlight the effectiveness of its strategies. These real-life examples bring a sense of relatability to the readers, making the strategies more believable and achievable. The case studies act as a mirror, reflecting the readers' own insecurities and uncertainties. By relating to the characters in the case studies, the readers are motivated to implement the strategies in their lives.

"Ditch the Uncertainty" is not just a book; it's a guide that helps its readers navigate their way through the maze of uncertainty. By providing practical strategies and illustrating them through real-life case studies, the book ensures that the readers are well equipped to tackle their uncertainties. It encourages its readers to believe in themselves and their decisions, thereby enabling them to live a life free of uncertainty.

The book provides a thorough analysis of each case study, explaining the strategies used and the resulting transformation. It offers a detailed breakdown of how each individual managed to ditch the uncertainty, providing a blueprint for readers to follow. By doing so, the book ensures that its readers are not just reading about the strategies but are also learning how to implement them in their lives.

"Ditch the Uncertainty" is more than just a self-help book; it's a tool that empowers its readers to take control of their lives. By providing practical strategies and real-life case studies, the book equips its readers with the necessary tools to conquer uncertainty, thereby enabling them to live a more confident and fulfilling life.

Lessons Learned

Navigating through the labyrinth of life, one is bound to stumble upon a multitude of lessons. These lessons, as diverse as they may be, serve as the guiding light, illuminating the path that lies ahead. They are the nuggets of wisdom gleaned from experiences; they are the pearls of wisdom that help to ditch the uncertainty.

Reflecting on the past, it is evident that every challenge, every hurdle, every setback, was nothing more than an opportunity in disguise. They were the stepping stones that paved the way for growth and development. It was during these times that the true strength and resilience were tested. The sheer determination and relentless pursuit of goals are what propelled forward, despite the odds. These lessons underscore the importance of perseverance and tenacity in the face of adversity.

One of the most profound lessons learned is the significance of adaptability. Change is the only constant in life, and being able to adapt to these changes is crucial. The ability to bend and not break under the pressure of change, to mold oneself according to the situation, is a skill of paramount importance. It is this adaptability that enables one to thrive in any environment, under any circumstances.

Another equally important lesson is the power of positivity. The mind is a powerful tool, and the thoughts that occupy it have a profound impact on the actions and the outcomes. Negative thoughts breed negativity, and positivity breeds positivity. Maintaining a positive outlook, even in the most challenging situations, has the power to transform the outcome. It is this positivity that serves as the beacon of hope in the darkest of times.

The significance of patience is yet another lesson learned. Success doesn't happen overnight. It is the result of persistent efforts and unwavering commitment. It is about staying the course, even when the progress seems slow or non-existent. Patience, coupled with determination, is the key that unlocks the door to success.

Yet, one of the most valuable lessons learned is the importance of self-belief. It is the unwavering faith in oneself, the belief in one's abilities, that fuels the drive to achieve goals. Doubt and uncertainty are the biggest obstacles on the path to success. It is the self-belief that helps to overcome these obstacles and propels forward.

The value of relationships is another lesson learned. No man is an island, and every individual is a part of the intricate web of relationships. These relationships, be it personal or professional, play a crucial role in shaping an individual. They provide the much-needed support, guidance, and motivation. They are the pillars on which one leans during the challenging times.

Life is a continuous learning process, and every experience, every encounter, every situation, teaches a lesson. These lessons are the stepping stones on the path to success. They are the guiding light that helps to ditch the uncertainty and navigate through the labyrinth of life with confidence and conviction. These lessons learned are not just the nuggets of wisdom, but the foundation on which the future is built.

Applying Case Study Insights

The application of insights gleaned from case studies is a critical step in overcoming uncertainty. The knowledge and understanding gained from these real-life examples can be a valuable tool in decision-making processes. This section will delve into how to effectively apply these insights to your own situation and experiences, helping you to navigate past the uncertainty and towards clearer, more confident decisions.

A case study is a detailed examination of a particular instance or situation, often involving complex problems or issues. The depth and detail of a case study allow for a comprehensive understanding of the situation, including the challenges faced, the strategies employed, and the outcomes achieved. These insights, when applied correctly, can illuminate potential solutions and provide a roadmap for action.

The first step in applying case study insights is understanding the context of the case. This involves identifying the key issues and challenges faced, as well as the strategies and tactics used to address them. It is important to understand not only what was done, but why it was done, and what the implications were. This understanding provides a solid foundation for applying the insights to your own situation.

Next, it is essential to translate the insights into actionable steps. This involves identifying the key elements that can be applied to your own situation and developing a plan of action. This may involve adapting strategies and tactics to fit your own context, or it may involve using the insights to generate new ideas and approaches.

A practical way to apply case study insights is through scenario planning. This involves envisioning different possible futures and developing strategies to navigate each one. The insights from case studies can be used to inform this process, helping to identify potential challenges and opportunities, and to develop effective strategies.

It is also important to reflect on the lessons learned from the case study. This involves not just understanding what happened, but also why it happened and what could be done differently. Reflecting on these lessons can help to identify potential pitfalls and to develop strategies to avoid them.

Another vital aspect of applying case study insights is continuous learning. This involves revisiting the case study and the insights derived from it, and updating your understanding and strategies as new information becomes available. Continuous learning allows for the ongoing refinement of strategies and tactics, and for the incorporation of new insights and information.

The application of case study insights is not a one-size-fits-all process. Each situation is unique, and the insights gained from one case may not be directly applicable to another. However, by understanding the context, translating insights into actionable steps, using scenario planning, reflecting on lessons learned, and engaging in continuous learning, it is possible to navigate past the uncertainty and towards more confident decisions.

Applying case study insights is a powerful tool in overcoming uncertainty. It allows for a deeper understanding of complex issues and provides a roadmap for action. By effectively applying these insights, you can ditch the uncertainty and move forward with confidence and clarity.

Case Studies in Action

We've explored strategies for tackling uncertainty, but theory only goes so far. This section dives into real-world examples – case studies that illustrate these strategies in action and showcase how uncertainty can be successfully overcome.

From Bricks to Clicks: Embracing Change

Imagine a small business owner facing a crossroads. His traditional brick-and-mortar store is struggling as consumer habits shift online. Uncertainty looms large – should he cling to the familiar or venture into the unknown digital world? Fear could easily paralyze him, but this entrepreneur takes a different approach.

He actively confronts uncertainty by seeking expert advice and studying successful online businesses. He uses the strategies discussed earlier – analyzing the situation, identifying weaknesses and opportunities, and formulating a plan. This proactive approach transforms his fear into a catalyst for change. He implements changes gradually, adapting his business model to the digital landscape. The result? A thriving online store, a testament to his courage to embrace the unknown.

A Multinational Giant Stands Tall

Now, let's shift gears to a corporate giant facing a different kind of uncertainty. Rapid market changes threaten to cripple the company. Profits plummet, and competition intensifies. Uncertainty breeds doubt – should they maintain the status quo or embark on a risky transformation?

The leadership demonstrates remarkable resolve. They choose not to succumb to fear but to confront uncertainty head-on. Following the principles outlined earlier, they conduct a comprehensive analysis of their operations, pinpointing areas for improvement and potential opportunities. They implement the discussed strategies, fostering a more adaptable and robust organization. This proactive approach equips them to weather the storm and emerge stronger.

Charting a Course: Finding Direction

Uncertainty can also plague personal decisions. A recent college graduate exemplifies this. With a vast array of career options before her, she feels overwhelmed and lost. Instead of succumbing to indecision, she takes control. She performs a self-assessment, identifying her strengths, passions, and career goals. By aligning her self-awareness with research on various career paths, she reduces the uncertainty and charts a clear course for a fulfilling professional journey.

These cases, along with countless others, underscore a crucial message: uncertainty can be conquered. The unifying thread in these stories is the willingness to confront the unknown. These individuals and organizations didn't shy away from the challenges; they analyzed them and formulated plans. They used uncertainty not as a roadblock, but as a motivator for positive change.

A Beacon of Hope

These case studies serve as a beacon of hope, illuminating a path through the fog of uncertainty. They demonstrate that with the right mindset and tools, we can not only manage uncertainty but even harness it for growth. The message is clear: confront uncertainty, analyze it, and take decisive action. By incorporating these principles, we can navigate the unknown with confidence and pave the way for a successful future, both personally and professionally.

CHAPTER 8
THRIVING IN THE LANDSCAPE OF EMERGING MARKETS

The Unpredictability Factor

Emerging markets thrum with an undeniable energy, a whirlwind of potential and pitfalls. For investors and entrepreneurs, this dynamism presents a captivating, yet often unnerving, reality. Just as meticulous planning seems to ensure success, unforeseen twists can send the best-laid strategies reeling.

The culprit? Unpredictability, the ever-present wild card that weaves uncertainty into the fabric of these markets. It's the invisible hand that shapes destinies, molding outcomes in ways no crystal ball could predict. Unexpected policy shifts, economic fluctuations, or social unrest can erupt, leaving even the most seasoned players disoriented and questioning their footing.

This inherent unpredictability can feel like a relentless foe, a force threatening to sweep away any semblance of control. But a closer look reveals a different truth: unpredictability is not just a challenge, but a catalyst. It's the nudge that propels businesses and investors out of comfortable routines, forcing them to adapt, innovate, and think on their feet.

Just as a spark ignites a fire, unpredictability sparks creativity. In the face of the unexpected, new solutions and strategies emerge. Companies must develop a keen ability to improvise, to explore uncharted territories, and to embrace new possibilities. This fosters a culture of resilience and resourcefulness, a vital asset in any emerging market.

The unpredictable nature of these markets is also undeniably exhilarating. It injects a dose of adventure into the oftenmundane world of finance. For those brave enough to navigate the unknown, the rewards can be substantial. Unforeseen opportunities can emerge, hidden gems waiting to be discovered by those with the courage to explore.

Yes, unpredictability can be unsettling. But it's also a potent reminder that the greatest rewards often lie beyond the comfort zone. It's the spice that seasons the investor's journey, the unexpected plot twist that keeps things interesting. So, instead of cowering in the face of the unknown, embrace it. Learn to dance to its rhythm, to ride its waves, and to find the magic that lies within the beautiful chaos.

Emerging markets are a testament to the fact that uncertainty is not a dead end, but a gateway. It's the threshold to discovery, the launchpad for innovation, and the key to unlocking the true potential that lies within the heart of the unexpected.

Adapting to Market Dynamics

The world of business is one that is constantly in flux, with market dynamics shifting like the sands of a desert. Entrepreneurs and business leaders must learn to adapt to these changes, or risk being left behind. The ability to adapt is not just about survival, but also about seizing opportunities and outpacing competitors.

In any business landscape, change is the only constant. Companies must learn to navigate through the ebb and flow of market demands, economic cycles, technological advancements, and regulatory shifts. These dynamics are not just external factors that businesses must respond to. They also shape the internal operations of a company, influencing strategy, decisionmaking, and even corporate culture.

Adaptation is not just about reacting to changes as they occur. It is also about anticipating future shifts and preparing for them. This requires constant vigilance and a keen understanding of the market. By closely monitoring industry trends, consumer behavior, and competitive activities, businesses can gain insights that help them anticipate future changes. This proactive approach allows them to stay ahead of the curve and make strategic decisions that position them for success.

Adaptation also involves flexibility. In a rapidly changing market, rigid strategies and business models can be a liability. Companies must be willing to pivot their strategies, restructure their operations, and reinvent their products or services to meet changing market demands. This might involve diversifying their product portfolio, entering new markets, or even radically changing their business model. While these shifts can be challenging, they can also open up new opportunities for growth and innovation.

A critical aspect of adaptation is resilience. Market dynamics can be unpredictable, and businesses may face setbacks and failures along the way. However, it is their ability to bounce back from these challenges that ultimately determines their success. Resilient businesses are those that can weather storms, learn from their mistakes, and emerge stronger and more competitive.

Adapting to market dynamics also involves a certain degree of risk-taking. Businesses must be willing to venture into the unknown, experiment with new ideas, and take calculated risks.

This entrepreneurial spirit is what drives innovation and progress. However, risk-taking should be balanced with sound judgment and strategic planning. Businesses must carefully evaluate the potential rewards and risks, and make informed decisions.

Adaptation is a continuous process that requires commitment and persistence. It is not a one-time event, but an ongoing journey of learning, experimenting, and evolving. Businesses must foster a culture of adaptation, where change is embraced as a part of daily operations. This involves fostering a mindset of curiosity, openness, and agility among employees, and equipping them with the skills and tools they need to adapt to changing market dynamics.

The ability to adapt to market dynamics is not just a survival skill, but a competitive advantage. Businesses that can swiftly and effectively adapt to changing market dynamics are more likely to thrive in the face of uncertainty, outperform their competitors, and achieve sustainable growth. In this everchanging business landscape, adaptation is not just an option, but a necessity.

Navigating Market Volatility

In the financial world, the term 'volatility' is often synonymous with risk, uncertainty, and even fear. It refers to the rapid and significant price movements that can occur in financial markets, such as stock, bond, and commodity markets. Despite its intimidating reputation, understanding and navigating market volatility is a critical component to successful investing.

One of the key aspects of navigating market volatility is understanding its nature. Volatility is not necessarily a bad thing. In fact, it is a normal part of market functioning and can offer opportunities for savvy investors. It is the very essence of markets, reflecting the constant ebb and flow of prices as market participants react to new information.

Volatility is often higher in bear markets, when investor sentiment is negative, and lower in bull markets, when sentiment is positive. However, it can also spike in response to specific events, such as economic data releases, corporate earnings announcements, or geopolitical events. This type of eventdriven volatility can be particularly challenging to navigate, as it can lead to rapid and significant price movements.

One of the most important tools in navigating market volatility is diversification. By spreading investments across a variety of asset classes, sectors, and geographic regions, investors can reduce their exposure to any single source of risk. Diversification can help to smooth out returns over time, reducing the impact of any single investment's performance on the overall portfolio.

Another key strategy is to maintain a long-term perspective. While short-term market movements can be unsettling, they are often just noise in the context of a long-term investment horizon. By focusing on long-term goals and maintaining a disciplined investment approach, investors can avoid making impulsive decisions based on short-term market fluctuations.

Risk management is also critical in navigating market volatility. This involves understanding the potential downside of each investment and taking steps to mitigate this risk. This could involve setting stop-loss orders to limit potential losses, using hedging strategies to protect against adverse price movements, or simply avoiding investments that are too risky.

While market volatility can be intimidating, it is important to remember that it is a normal part of investing. By understanding its nature, diversifying investments, maintaining a long-term perspective, and implementing effective risk management strategies, investors can navigate market volatility and potentially even turn it to their advantage.

It is also worth noting that market volatility is not always a sign of underlying economic or financial instability. Often, it simply reflects the fact that markets are constantly adjusting to new information. This is a healthy and necessary part of market functioning.

In the unpredictable world of investing, volatility is one of the few constants. However, with the right strategies and mindset, investors can navigate market volatility and use it to their advantage. While it may be tempting to shy away from volatile markets, doing so could mean missing out on potential investment opportunities. By embracing volatility as a normal part of investing, investors can position themselves to succeed in any market environment.

Emerging Market Success Stories

The global economic landscape is a vast and ever-evolving tapestry, with emerging markets emerging as vibrant hubs for enterprising businesses. These markets, characterized by rapid growth and development, pulsate with potential for those bold enough to navigate their complexities. Let's embark on a journey to explore some of the remarkable success stories woven into the fabric of these exciting economies.

Alibaba: A Jack Ma-de Success Story

Our expedition begins with Alibaba, a Chinese e-commerce giant that has become a global leader. This behemoth, birthed from the vision of Jack Ma, a former English teacher, started as a humble online marketplace. Through continuous innovation and a keen understanding of the Chinese consumer, Alibaba has blossomed to encompass retail, entertainment, and technology sectors. Their success hinges on their ability to tailor solutions to the unique needs of their audience, proving that local knowledge is a potent weapon in the global marketplace.

Reliance Jio: Revolutionizing India, One Connection at a Time

Shifting our focus to the Indian subcontinent, we encounter Reliance Jio, a telecommunications powerhouse that has revolutionized the industry. Launched in 2016, Jio disrupted the market by offering blazing-fast 4G services at remarkably low prices. This audacious strategy not only attracted a tidal wave of users, but also forced competitors to adapt, ultimately propelling India's digital transformation.

MercadoLibre: The Latin American E-commerce Kingpin

Latin America boasts its own champion – MercadoLibre, often dubbed the "Amazon of South America." This e-commerce titan has outshone its global counterparts by prioritizing local needs and preferences. From crafting payment solutions suited to cash-based economies to tackling infrastructure challenges through logistics investments, MercadoLibre's localized approach has been the cornerstone of its success.

Safaricom: M-Pesa – Banking on Innovation in Africa

Africa too, has its share of success stories. Safaricom, a Kenyan telecommunications company, has made a significant impact with its mobile money service, M-Pesa. Launched in 2007, MPesa has transformed Kenya's financial landscape by providing a safe and convenient way to send and receive money, particularly for those without access to traditional banking. M-Pesa's success has inspired similar initiatives across the globe, proving the power of innovation in addressing local challenges.

Lessons Learned: More Than Just a Story

These remarkable narratives illuminate the immense potential that lies within emerging markets. However, they also highlight the crucial role of local context. Each of these companies achieved success not by mimicking strategies from developed markets, but by crafting innovative solutions specific to their unique environments.

Navigating the Rapids: Challenges and Considerations

It's important to acknowledge that success in emerging markets is not a guaranteed outcome. These landscapes are often marked by volatility, regulatory uncertainties, and fierce competition. Businesses must be prepared to adapt quickly and continuously innovate to stay afloat. Furthermore, success in one emerging market doesn't automatically translate to another. Each market has its own ecosystem, cultural nuances, and consumer preferences. Therefore, a deep understanding of the local landscape, coupled with a flexible and adaptable business strategy, is paramount.

The stories of Alibaba, Reliance Jio, MercadoLibre, and Safaricom serve as testaments to the immense opportunities that emerging markets offer. They are powerful reminders that with the right approach, businesses can not only survive but thrive in these dynamic and often unpredictable environments. So, for those seeking to expand their horizons and conquer new frontiers, emerging markets beckon with the promise of adventure, reward, and a chance to be a part of the next big story.

CHAPTER 9
THE FUTURE OF INVESTING IN EMERGING MARKETS

Market Trends and Predictions

The business landscape, particularly in emerging markets, is a dynamic ocean, constantly churning with change and opportunity. Forecasting market trends is a vital skill for businesses seeking to stay afloat in these ever-shifting currents. This involves a keen eye for market behavior, the ability to identify patterns, and the strategic use of this knowledge to predict future directions.

The digital revolution has undoubtedly reshaped market trends in emerging economies. The rise of e-commerce, social media, and digital marketing has fundamentally altered how businesses operate and connect with consumers. Today's empowered consumers have more control over purchasing decisions than ever before, thanks to the vast amount of information readily available online. Businesses must acknowledge and adapt to this shift in power, prioritizing customer experience and building strong online presences.

Artificial Intelligence (AI) and Machine Learning (ML) are also playing a transformative role. These technologies are used to analyze consumer behavior, predict trends, and personalize marketing strategies. Businesses that fail to integrate AI and ML risk falling behind in this tech-driven era.

Sustainability is another major trend gaining momentum. Emerging market consumers are increasingly environmentally conscious, demanding businesses operate with a similar focus. This has led to a surge in demand for sustainable products and practices. Businesses that disregard sustainability risk alienating a significant portion of their customer base.

It's important to remember that market trends are fluid. Predictions, while valuable, should be approached with caution. However, by analyzing current trends and historical data, we can make some educated guesses about the future.

Here are some key predictions for future market trends in emerging economies:

The Digital Revolution's Continued Dominance: Technological advancements will necessitate continuous updates to digital strategies. This includes strengthening online presence, implementing effective digital marketing strategies, and embracing AI and ML for enhanced operations.

The Rise of the Empowered Consumer: Fueled by social media and online reviews, consumers will wield even greater influence. Businesses must prioritize customer satisfaction and engagement for sustained success.

Sustainability as a Cornerstone: Environmental concerns will continue to escalate, demanding demonstrably sustainable business practices. This may involve implementing eco-friendly production processes, sourcing sustainable materials, or developing environmentally conscious products.

Agility and Adaptability Take Center Stage: Unpredictability is becoming the norm. Businesses need to be agile and adaptable, prepared to react swiftly to changing market dynamics. This could involve product diversification, market expansion, or adopting innovative business models.

Understanding and predicting market trends is a complex but crucial endeavor for businesses operating in emerging markets. By constantly monitoring the market landscape, identifying patterns, and leveraging this knowledge for strategic decision making, businesses can anticipate change, adapt effectively, and ultimately, navigate the uncertainties of the market with confidence.

Emerging Technologies and Their Impact

As we delve into the heart of the digital revolution, we encounter a host of emerging technologies that are reshaping the world as we know it. These technologies—ranging from artificial intelligence and robotics to Blockchain and the Internet of Things (IoT)—are not only altering the way we live and work, but also upending traditional industries and creating new ones in their wake.

Artificial intelligence (AI), for instance, is no longer the stuff of science fiction. It is fast becoming an integral part of our everyday lives. From Google's search algorithms and Facebook's news feed to Amazon's shopping recommendations and Apple's Siri, AI is everywhere. It is being used to drive cars, diagnose diseases, personalize learning, and even write news articles. In the business world, AI is helping companies make sense of vast amounts of data, improve efficiency, and gain a competitive edge.

Similarly, robotics is revolutionizing sectors as diverse as manufacturing, healthcare, agriculture, and logistics. Robots are not only taking over mundane and repetitive tasks but also performing complex operations that require precision and consistency. In the healthcare sector, for instance, surgical robots are helping doctors perform minimally invasive surgeries with greater accuracy and less risk. In agriculture, drones are being used for precision farming and crop monitoring.

Blockchain, on the other hand, is promising to bring about a new era of transparency, security, and efficiency. Originally developed as the underlying technology for Bitcoin, Blockchain has potential applications far beyond cryptocurrencies. It is being used to create tamper-proof records, streamline supply chains, verify identities, protect intellectual property, and much more. Blockchain could also change the way we vote, by making elections more secure and transparent.

The Internet of Things (IoT) is another game-changing technology that is connecting the physical and digital worlds in unprecedented ways. From smart homes and wearable devices to connected cars and smart cities, IoT is enabling a new level of automation, efficiency, and convenience. It is also generating massive amounts of data that can be used to gain insights and make informed decisions.

However, these emerging technologies are not without their challenges and risks. They raise important questions about privacy, security, ethics, and governance. They also have the potential to disrupt jobs and exacerbate inequality. For instance, the widespread adoption of AI and robotics could lead to job displacement and skill mismatches. Similarly, the proliferation of IoT devices could create new vulnerabilities and privacy concerns.

Moreover, these technologies are not developing in isolation. They are converging and interacting in complex ways, creating a whole that is greater than the sum of its parts. AI, for instance, is powering the development of autonomous robots and smart IoT devices. Blockchain, on the other hand, could provide a secure and transparent framework for IoT transactions.

In this fast-paced and ever-evolving landscape, it is crucial for individuals, businesses, and societies to understand and adapt to these technologies. They need to harness their potential, mitigate their risks, and navigate their challenges. They also need to rethink their strategies, structures, and skills to thrive in the digital age.

In the face of uncertainty, one thing is clear: these emerging technologies are not just shaping the future—they are the future. And those who fail to recognize and respond to this reality risk being left behind.

The Role of Governments and Policies

In a world characterized by constant flux, where uncertainty seems to be the only certainty, there are few entities that hold as much sway as governments and the policies they institute. These governing bodies, in their various forms, can be seen as the helmsmen of our collective ship, steering us through the turbulent sea of unpredictability. It is through their actions, decisions, and the policies they enact that the course of nations and, by extension, the world is charted.

Governments serve as the custodians of order, the architects of societal frameworks, and the arbiters of justice. They are tasked with the responsibility of maintaining stability and fostering an environment conducive to growth and prosperity. This is achieved through the implementation of policies that seek to regulate, guide, and influence various aspects of societal life, from the economy and the environment, to education and healthcare.

Policies, in essence, are the tools with which governments sculpt the societal landscape. They are the directives that shape the contours of our collective existence and determine the direction in which we move. They are the levers that governments pull to bring about change, to respond to crises, and to guide the course of development. Policies are the means through which governments seek to provide answers to the pressing questions of the day and offer solutions to the challenges that we face.

In the face of uncertainty, the role of governments and their policies becomes even more critical. It is during these times of ambiguity and unpredictability that the need for clear, decisive action and guidance is most acutely felt. It is in these moments that the ability of governments to provide stability, reassurance, and direction is put to the test.

Consider, for example, the economic uncertainty that often accompanies periods of political turmoil. In such instances, it is the economic policies of governments – their decisions regarding interest rates, taxation, and public spending – that can either alleviate the situation or exacerbate it. Similarly, in the face of environmental uncertainty, it is the environmental policies of governments – their stance on issues like climate change, conservation, and renewable energy – that can determine the trajectory of our shared future.

However, the role of governments and policies extends beyond merely responding to uncertainty. They are also instrumental in creating an environment in which uncertainty can be managed and navigated. Through policies that promote education, innovation, and resilience, governments can equip individuals and societies with the tools they need to face the unknown. They can foster a culture of adaptability and flexibility, encouraging us to see uncertainty not merely as a threat, but as an opportunity for growth and development.

In a world characterized by uncertainty, governments and their policies play a crucial role. They are the compass that guides us through the murky waters of unpredictability, the anchor that provides us with stability, and the beacon that lights the way forward. They have the power to shape our collective response to uncertainty and influence the manner in which we navigate its challenges. It is through their actions and decisions that we find the courage to ditch the uncertainty and embrace the possibilities that lie ahead.

Investor's Role in Shaping the Future

Investors, whether they are individuals or institutions, play a pivotal role in shaping the future of our world. Their influence extends much beyond the financial sphere and into the realms of technology, society and the environment. Their decisions, often driven by foresight and acumen, act as catalysts in setting the trajectory for progress and development.

Investors, by their very nature, are visionaries. They see potential where others see risk. They see the future in the present. Their choices, therefore, are not just about immediate gains but also about long-term impact. They are the ones who are willing to support new ideas, technologies, and businesses that have the potential to transform our lives and our world.

The power of the investor lies in their ability to fuel innovation. They provide the much-needed capital to entrepreneurs and businesses, enabling them to turn their ideas into reality. Through their investments, they support the development of new products and services, which can revolutionize industries and change the way we live.

Moreover, investors have a significant role in driving societal change. By choosing to invest in companies that align with their values, they can influence corporate behavior. For instance, an increasing number of investors are now supporting companies that prioritize sustainability and social responsibility. This trend is driving more businesses to adopt environmentally friendly practices and contribute positively to society.

Investors also play a crucial role in shaping the economic landscape. Their investment decisions help determine which industries and sectors thrive and which ones decline. They can steer economies towards growth and prosperity by investing in sectors that have the potential for high returns and job creation.

The investor's role in shaping the future also extends to the realm of policy-making. By lobbying for favorable policies and regulations, they can create an environment conducive to business growth and innovation. They can influence government decisions on issues such as taxation, trade, and regulation, which can have far-reaching implications for the economy and society.

However, with great power comes great responsibility. While investors have the potential to shape the future positively, they can also contribute to problems if they prioritize short-term gains over long-term sustainability. Therefore, it is crucial for investors to exercise their power responsibly and consider the broader implications of their decisions.

Investors are not just passive players in the game of wealth creation. They are active participants in shaping the future of our world. Their decisions can have a profound impact on our lives and our planet. Hence, it is essential for them to recognize their role and make investment decisions that contribute to a sustainable and prosperous future.

In the uncertain world that we live in, investors can provide a sense of direction. By backing the right ideas and businesses, they can help navigate the path towards growth and progress. Therefore, the role of investors in shaping the future cannot be underestimated.

In this ever-evolving world, it is the investors who hold the key to the future. Their decisions today will determine the course of our world tomorrow. By recognizing their role and acting responsibly, they can contribute to a future that is not only prosperous but also sustainable and equitable.

CHAPTER 10
CONCLUSION: DITCHING THE UNCERTAINTY

Recap and Key Takeaways

Reflecting on the initial chapters of "Ditch the Uncertainty," we find ourselves brimming with insights and revelations. The book has started the process of deconstructing the complex web of uncertainty that often clouds our minds and prevents us from reaching our full potential. We have begun to understand the essence of clarity and how it can be a powerful tool in our hands.

The initial chapters have shed light on the fact that uncertainty is not an external force, but an internal condition that we often impose on ourselves. We have learned that it stems from our fears, insecurities, and lack of confidence. It is a result of our hesitations and doubts about our capabilities. The book has made us realize that to overcome uncertainty, we need to start by acknowledging these negative feelings and then work towards eliminating them.

One of the key takeaways from the initial chapters is the understanding that uncertainty is not always bad. It has been portrayed not as a villain but as a catalyst that can spur us into action. It can make us question our beliefs and assumptions, thereby leading to personal growth and development. The book has emphasized that it is how we respond to uncertainty that determines its impact on our lives.

Another major insight that the book has provided is the importance of self-confidence in combating uncertainty. Selfconfidence, as the book has explained, is not a trait that some people are born with and others are not. It is a skill that can be developed and strengthened. The book has given us practical tips and strategies to build our self-confidence, such as setting realistic goals, celebrating small victories, and learning from our failures.

The book has also touched upon the role of decision-making in dealing with uncertainty. It has stressed that making decisions, even if they turn out to be wrong, is better than staying stuck in a state of indecision. The book has taught us that every decision, good or bad, brings us one step closer to clarity.

Moreover, the book has underscored the significance of resilience in the face of uncertainty. It has shown us that resilience is not about avoiding uncertainty but about facing it head-on and bouncing back from it. The book has encouraged us to see uncertainty as a challenge to be overcome rather than a problem to be feared.

In addition, the book has highlighted the need for adaptability in today's ever-changing world. It has pointed out that those who can adapt to new situations and circumstances are better equipped to handle uncertainty. The book has urged us to be open to change and be willing to step out of our comfort zones.

In the realm of uncertainty, the book has also introduced the concept of 'calculated risks.' It has explained that taking calculated risks can lead to extraordinary rewards. The book has advised us to weigh the pros and cons before taking a risk and to be prepared for the consequences.

In essence, "Ditch the Uncertainty" has laid the groundwork for us to understand and manage uncertainty. It has equipped us with the knowledge and tools to transform uncertainty from a stumbling block into a stepping stone. As we continue to delve deeper into the book, we look forward to gaining more insights and learning more strategies to deal with uncertainty.

Empowering Yourself as an Investor

The allure of financial freedom beckons, and emerging markets offer a landscape teeming with potential. But unlocking this potential requires you, the investor, to seize the reins. This journey to empowerment is paved with knowledge, unwavering confidence, and the ability to take calculated risks. This guide equips you with the tools and techniques to become a selfreliant investor in the dynamic world of emerging markets.

Building Your Financial Fortress: Knowledge is Power

The first step is to establish a sturdy foundation. Educate yourself on the diverse investment options available, from stocks and bonds to real estate and alternative investments. Stay abreast of market trends and economic news. Remember, the goal isn't to become a financial guru overnight, but to cultivate a continuous learning mindset. Numerous online resources, books, and workshops can be your allies in this quest for financial literacy.

Sharpening Your Analytical Edge: Question Everything

Don't be a passive investor; become an active analyst. Develop the crucial skill of critical thinking. Don't blindly accept information – delve deeper to understand the underlying factors influencing market movements. For example, don't just chase a hot stock; scrutinize its success and assess its alignment with your investment goals. This ability to dissect information empowers you to make well-informed decisions, safeguarding you from impulsive, emotion-driven choices.

Taming the Risk Beast: Mastering the Art of Risk Management

Risk is an inevitable companion in the investment world, but it shouldn't paralyze you. Learn to manage it like a skilled tamer. Diversification is your shield – spread your investments across various asset classes to mitigate losses in any single sector. Employ stop-loss limits to automatically sell under-performing assets, and regularly review your portfolio to maintain a healthy balance between potential returns and potential losses. Remember, the goal is not to eliminate risk entirely, but to control it to a level you're comfortable navigating.

Setting Your Sights: Define Your Investment Goals

Empowered investors have a clear road-map. Define your investment goals, whether it's securing a dream retirement, acquiring a home, or building an emergency fund. Having a specific target in mind provides direction. It informs your choice of investment options and keeps you motivated during inevitable market fluctuations.

Confidence is Your Compass: Trust Your Judgment

Confidence is the cornerstone of investor empowerment. It doesn't equate to overconfidence, but rather a healthy belief in your abilities. Trust your judgment, even when opinions differ.

The courage to take calculated risks stems from a foundation of knowledge, practical experience, and a positive mindset. So, keep learning, gain experience by putting your knowledge into practice, and cultivate a positive outlook towards investing.

Seeking Guidance, Not Dependence: A Helping Hand

The path to self-reliance doesn't necessitate a solitary journey. Financial advisors can offer valuable insights, particularly in complex situations. However, remember to view their advice as a guiding light, not a set of rigid instructions. The ultimate decision always rests with you.

Empowerment: A Continuous Journey

Empowerment is not a destination, but a continuous odyssey of learning, adapting, and making informed decisions. As your selfreliance grows, you'll witness not only a positive impact on your investments, but also a profound sense of control and satisfaction that comes from steering your financial future. Equip yourself with the right tools, cultivate the right mindset, and embark on your journey to conquer the emerging markets with confidence.

The Journey Ahead

Step into the Uncharted: Opportunity Awaits

The narrative unfolds, each page drawing you deeper into the captivating realm of emerging markets. Here, opportunity and challenge are intricately woven, beckoning the adventurous investor. This is not a physical voyage, but an intellectual and audacious one, a quest to shed the veil of the unknown and unlock the secrets of these dynamic economies.

Embrace the Mystery: Where Growth Lies

A veil of uncertainty hangs in the air, shrouding the path ahead. Yet, within this ambiguity lies the catalyst for your success: unwavering resolve, unwavering courage, and an insatiable thirst for knowledge. It is here, in the crucible of the unknown, that you transform, pushing past self-imposed limitations and embracing the boundless potential for growth.

Forge Your Path: Lessons Learned, Victories Earned

The road ahead is not paved with gold, but with invaluable experiences waiting to be unearthed. Each triumph and every stumble shapes you into the astute investor you aspire to be. You are not merely a collection of experiences, but rather the sum of your insightful reactions to them.

Chart Your Course: The Captain of Your Destiny

This uncharted territory is yours to navigate. As the architect of your own destiny, you captain your course with unwavering determination. The compass of your investment strategy rests firmly in your grasp, guiding you towards the realization of your financial goals. Though the terrain may be unfamiliar and the ascent demanding, your unwavering resolve and resilience will be your guiding light.

Standing on the Shoulders of Giants: A Legacy of Knowledge

You are not a lone voyager on this odyssey. The echoes of those who ventured before resonate still, their wisdom carried on the wind, their lessons etched in the sands of time. From their triumphs, you draw strength, and from their missteps, invaluable knowledge. You are but one link in the chain of human endeavor, a testament to the collective spirit that transcends generations.

Tempered by Adversity: Where True Strength Lies

This venture is not without its trials. Obstacles will rise, setbacks will test your mettle, and your deepest fears and insecurities may surface. However, it is through these very challenges that you discover the depths of your strength and resourcefulness. Adversity serves as the crucible that forges your investment acumen, where your resolve is tested and your confidence is solidified.

Empowered by Knowledge: A Well-Stocked Arsenal

You are equipped for this journey. Weary not, for you carry with you a well-stocked arsenal of knowledge, skills, and experiences, each element playing a vital role in your quest for financial success. You are not ill-prepared but rather empowered, ready to face whatever may unfold on this exciting adventure. We are not pawns of circumstance, but the masters of our own financial destiny.

Moments of Doubt: A Determined Spirit Prevails

Moments of doubt will inevitably arise, whispers of fear threatening to derail your progress. Yet, in these moments, remember the spark that ignited your journey – your ambition, your passion, and your unwavering vision. You are not defined by the challenges you face, but by the unwavering spirit with which you overcome them.

A Mission of Discovery: Beyond Uncertainty

This venture is a testament to your relentless spirit, your unwavering resilience, and your unwavering determination to shed the cloak of uncertainty. You are not merely embarking on a journey; you are on a mission. A mission to explore the uncharted territories of emerging markets, to forge your own path to financial freedom, and to seize control of your destiny.

The story that unfolds is a collaborative masterpiece, but with an added layer of security. Curaçao's robust Bilateral Investment Treaty (BIT) network serves as a valuable ingredient in your recipe for success. These treaties provide a legal framework that protects your investments and fosters a climate of trust and stability. Together, with the expertise of BIT in Curaçao at your side, you are empowered to make informed decisions and navigate the complexities of emerging markets with greater confidence.

This journey is yours to author, with each strategic decision shaping your narrative. The path that lies ahead is yours to tread, guided by the expertise of BIT in Curaçao. Together, you will unlock the boundless potential of emerging markets and transform uncertainty into a resounding success story.

Final Words of Advice

As we reach the summit of this enlightening expedition, a truth becomes crystal clear: the path to conquering uncertainty isn't a straight line. It's a winding trail, occasionally obscured by challenges unique to each traveler. Yet, with the right tools and a determined spirit, you possess the power to navigate the fog and emerge into a landscape of unwavering confidence.

The strategies within these pages are your compass, not a magic map. They demand patience, unwavering dedication, and a willingness to shed limiting beliefs. Stepping outside your comfort zone is inevitable, and so is resilience in the face of setbacks. Remember, courage fuels the pursuit of your goals.

The journey begins with a single, resolute step. Take control of your life, and relinquish the reins to fear and doubt. Embrace the realization that you, not circumstance, are the architect of your destiny.

Be kind to yourself throughout this odyssey. Mistakes are stepping stones, not roadblocks. It's okay to feel fear, and even seek help. We're all human, navigating the best we can.

Conquering uncertainty doesn't mean eliminating doubt and fear. It signifies control, the ability to confront them head-on and fuel your growth.

Now, venture forth, armed with newfound knowledge and a resolute spirit. Trust in your capabilities. You are stronger than you imagine, capable of overcoming any obstacle.

When uncertainty looms, find your center. Breathe. Take it one step at a time. Celebrate victories, big or small. Most importantly, believe in yourself.

Remember, as you depart, the only constant is change. So, instead of fearing the unknown, embrace its potential. Let it propel you forward, a catalyst for growth. Uncertainty is not a villain, but a teacher, an opportunity in disguise.

Learn to live with it, even thrive alongside it. Ultimately, transform it into your greatest asset.

This book is your companion on your path to unshakeable confidence. May it inspire you to ditch uncertainty and embrace a life brimming with courage and self-assuredness. As you embark on this extraordinary journey, remember, you have everything you need to succeed. Now go forth and conquer.